FISHING BASICS

by John Randolph

Illustrated by
Art Seiden

•

Photographs by
John Randolph

•

Created and produced by
Arvid Knudsen

•

Prentice-Hall, Inc.

Englewood Cliffs, New Jersey

Dedication

To my loving parents.

Other **Sports Basics Books** in Series

BASKETBALL BASICS *by Greggory Morris*
RUNNING BASICS *by Carol Lea Benjamin*
DISCO BASICS *by Maxine Polley*
GYMNASTICS BASICS *by John and Mary Jean Traetta*
RACQUETBALL BASICS *by Tony Boccaccio*
FRISBEE DISC BASICS *by Dan Roddick*
SWIMMING BASICS *by Rob Orr and Jane B. Tyler*
HORSEBACK RIDING BASICS *by Dianne Reimer*
SKIING BASICS *by Al Morrozzi*
BASEBALL BASICS *by Jack Lang*
FOOTBALL BASICS *by Larry Fox*

Book design by Arvid Knudsen

Printed in the United States of America   ·J

Prentice-Hall International, Inc., London
Prentice-Hall of Australia, Pty. Ltd., North Sydney
Prentice-Hall of Canada, Ltd., Toronto
Prentice-Hall of India Private Ltd., New Delhi
Prentice-Hall of Japan, Inc., Tokyo
Prentice-Hall of Southeast Asia Pte. Ltd., Singapore
Whitehall Books Limited, Wellington, New Zealand

10 9 8 7 6 5 4 3 2

Library of Congress Cataloging in Publication Data

Randolph, John D.
 Fishing basics.

 Summary: Introduces one of mankind's oldest
activities, focusing on fishing as a sport. Discusses
types of fish and strategies and locations for catching
them.
  1. Fishing—Juvenile literature. [1. Fishing]
I. Knudsen, ARvid. II. Title.
SH445.R36   799.1   81-8698
ISBN 0-13-319707-7   AACR2
ISBN 0-13-319732-8 (pbk.)

CONTENTS

Preface

Catching your first fish can be an unforgettable moment of excitement, so captivating that you may even continue fishing for the rest of your life to recapture the same thrill. Fishing may also become a lifelong road to learning and adventure for you. After all, fish are part of the natural world, and they live in the most beautiful and unspoiled spots on our planet.

This book is my invitation to you. Come learn about fish and how to catch them. I can help you begin this adventure, but although we begin together, you must truly do the wonderful searching and learning yourself. If you like fishing the way I do, you'll haunt the places where fish are found. You'll like what you find there.

John Randolph

1

THE SPORT OF FISHING

Why do 60 million people each year try to catch fish on hooks and lines? Each fisherman finds his own challenge and reason to fish. Here are some:

1. *If you've ever tried to catch a butterfly on the wing or a green frog jumping in the grass, then you know the fascination of trying to catch something live. You will probably enjoy the thrill of watching a fishing bobber nod and dip underwater at the tug of a fish.*

2. *You may feel the challenge of fooling a wild fish into biting what is on your hook. It's an excitement all true fishermen feel, an urge that gets them up before dawn to fish.*

3. *Some fishermen want to catch the biggest fish, which will become a trophy to hang on their wall as a memento of their accomplishment.*

4. *For others fishing is a quiet sport, away from the noise and bustle of the city, where they can relax while waiting for a fish to bite.*

5. *Some fishermen fish to bring home food for their families. For others, catching the most fish is as exciting as scoring the most points in a basketball game.*

Where to Fish and How to Learn

What's the best way to find where to fish and to learn how?

Fishing is a solitary sport: it's you against the fish. But, as in all sports, the best way to learn is to begin when you are young. Begin as close to home as you can, and begin your fishing with an experienced fisherman who can teach you.

8

To learn fishing you must fish. Your first fishing trip may be just an afternoon walk to a neighborhood pond, dock, or lake; but if you find fishermen there, ask questions. They will explain what they are doing and how they are doing it. Fishermen like to share the secrets about their sport. You'll like the people you meet fishing. They enjoy their sport and they like to help others enjoy it too.

The Language of Fishing

All sports have a special language of their own. So it is with fishing. Before we go any further in our basics book, there are some basic fishing terms you should become immediately acquainted with. The sport of fishing is really quite vast. It gets very technical the more you advance. But first, become familiar with the following words and expressions. Then refer to our Glossary of Terms at the back of the book for further understanding of terms you will encounter throughout the forthcoming chapters.

The following terms are among the most important to know in order to be introduced to fishing:

Bait: The three types of bait are 1. live, 2. artificial, and 3. fresh. Live bait are live things that swim, crawl, or fly, such as worms, nightcrawlers, minnows, or flies. Artificial baits imitate live baits (lures, etc.). Fresh bait is cutup live material, such as pieces of fish, clams, or worms.

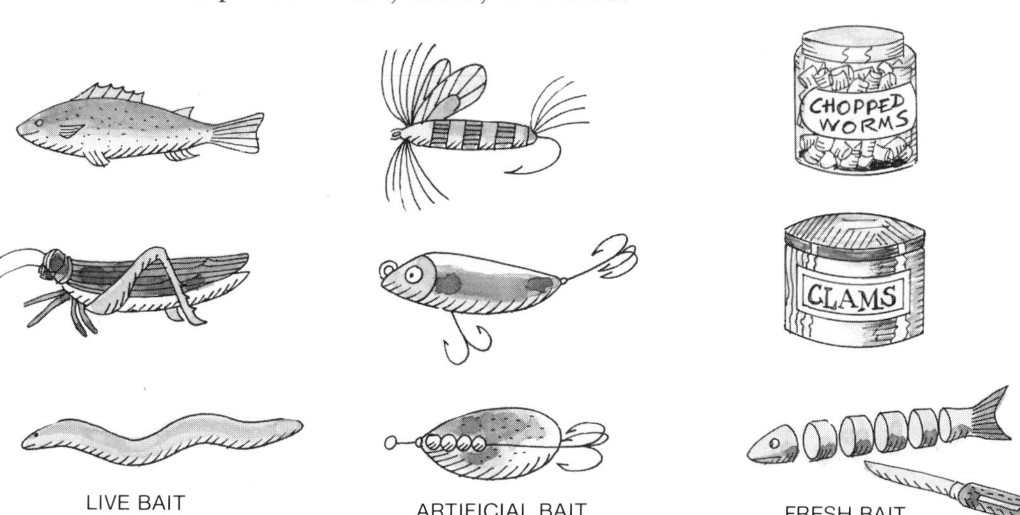

9

Bait box: A box used to hold bait, particularly live bait such as worms and nightcrawlers.

Cast: The arm motion used to throw a bait or lure with a fishing rod.

Drop line: The simplest fishing rig used by fishermen—a hook and line wrapped on a small wood or plastic frame.

Fish net: A hand net used to complete the capture of a fish once it has been hooked and "played"—fought until tired. Large boat nets are used for large fish; small ones are used for small fish.

Fly-fishing: Fishing that uses bits of feathers and tinsel tied on hooks to imitate insects and other bait fish feed on.

Gaff: A large hook used to catch a fish once it has been brought to the boat.

Land: To catch a fish by bringing it to a net or gaff.

Freshwater rainbow trout jumping the falls to run up river to spawn. Female fish lay their eggs in the stream's gravel where they are fertilized by the male.

2
WHAT FISH ARE

Fish are creatures that live in water. They take air from the water by passing it through their gills. No matter where they live, fish need clean water and food to survive. Most of a fish's life is spent pursuing food or being pursued for food by a larger fish. Both freshwater and saltwater fish have developed special senses to survive in their water world, senses that might surprise you.

Most fish are *predators*—they feed on other fish, insects, and shellfish that will fit into their mouths. To find these foods, fish need a good sense of smell and good underwater eyesight and hearing to sense underwater sounds. Fish also have noses that are sensitive to smells in water. For instance, Atlantic salmon—fish that return to freshwater streams from the ocean to spawn—have noses so sensitive that they can smell the waters where they were born after being away in the ocean for two years or more.

A fish can sense vibrations in the water through a sensitive nerve in its side; so in fishing you should be careful about loud thumps on your boat or splashing when wading in a stream. The noises that sound in water will frighten the fish, and they won't feed on your bait.

Fish are sensitive to movement, and because they are hungry most of the time and find their food by spotting it when it moves, fishermen use foods that move the way a fish expects them to. This movement excites the fish into biting a hook.

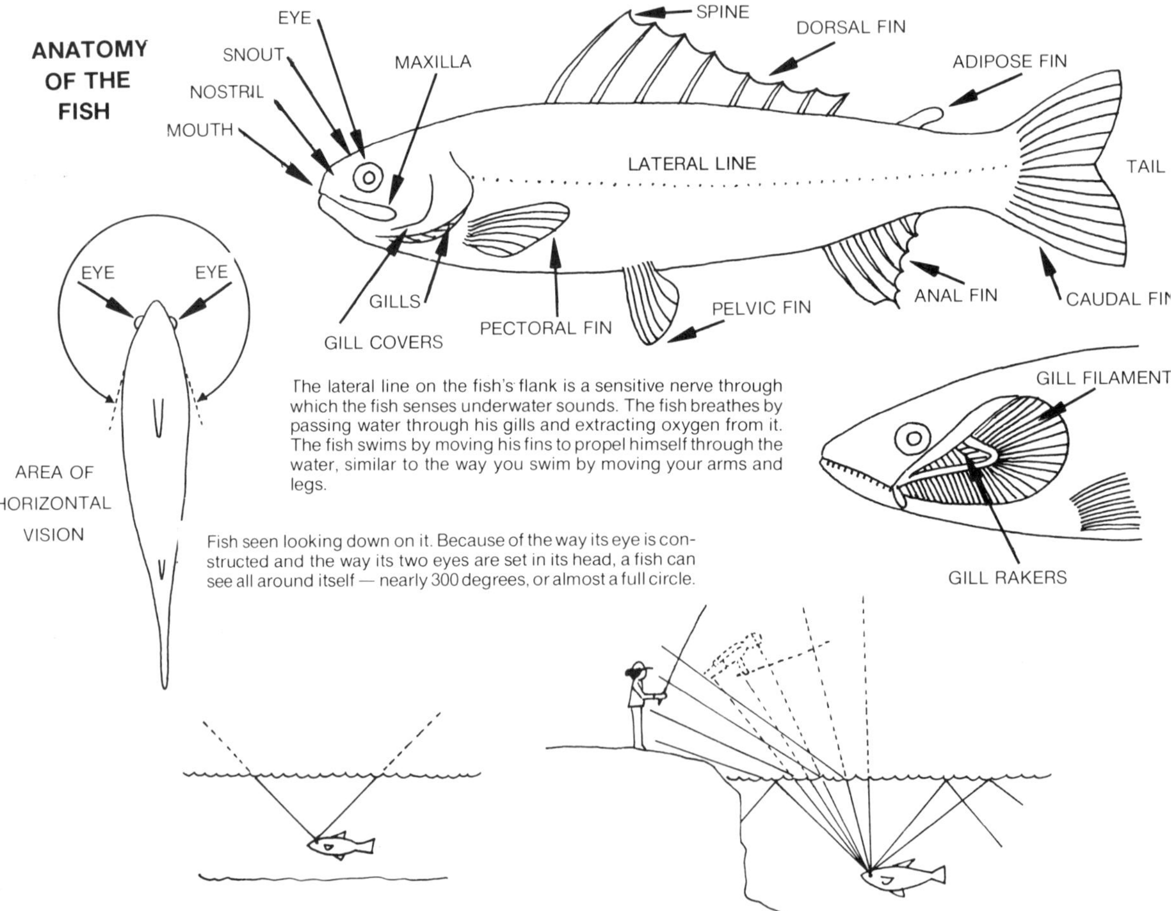

The lateral line on the fish's flank is a sensitive nerve through which the fish senses underwater sounds. The fish breathes by passing water through his gills and extracting oxygen from it. The fish swims by moving his fins to propel himself through the water, similar to the way you swim by moving your arms and legs.

Fish seen looking down on it. Because of the way its eye is constructed and the way its two eyes are set in its head, a fish can see all around itself — nearly 300 degrees, or almost a full circle.

When a fish looks upward the water's surface reflects the light from the sky down at sharp angles so the fish can see only 90 degrees.

So what a fish often sees when you approach a stream bank is a tilted view of you. To approach without being seen by fish you much crouch or crawl.

Types of Fish

You will find fish almost everywhere you find water. To make things easy, let's consider fish that live in fresh water and then those that make salt water their home.

FRESHWATER FISH

Freshwater fish came to land millions of years ago from the sea. Slowly they learned to live in salt-free waters; and today they live in rivers, ponds, lakes, streams, and in impoundments made by man for his drinking water and irrigation. The freshwater fish are also called "coldwater fish" or "warmwater fish." In other words, some freshwater fish need cold water in which to live, while others need warm water to survive. Let's look at some kinds of fish and where to find them—in what we call their "habitat."

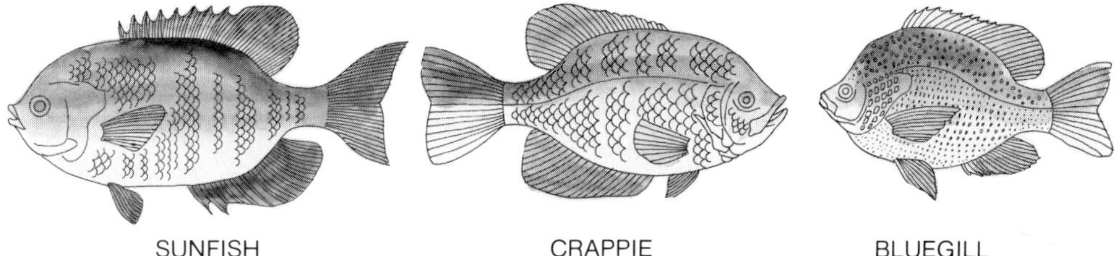

I learned to fish in little ponds where the warm water was full of "panfish." These little fish live in virtually every warmwater pond. They have such names as sunfish, bluegill, perch, crappie, and bream; and they are good to eat.

You can lie on your stomach on a boat dock and dangle a fishline, hook, and worm in the water and catch panfish one after another. If there's a pond near your home, you can bet there will be panfish in it.

There may be other larger warmwater fish in the ponds and lakes near your home. A good panfish angler often graduates to fishing for these large fish that feed on the panfish. Largemouth and smallmouth bass, northern pike, chain pickerel, and walleyed pike are exciting to catch because they are large and are hard fighters.

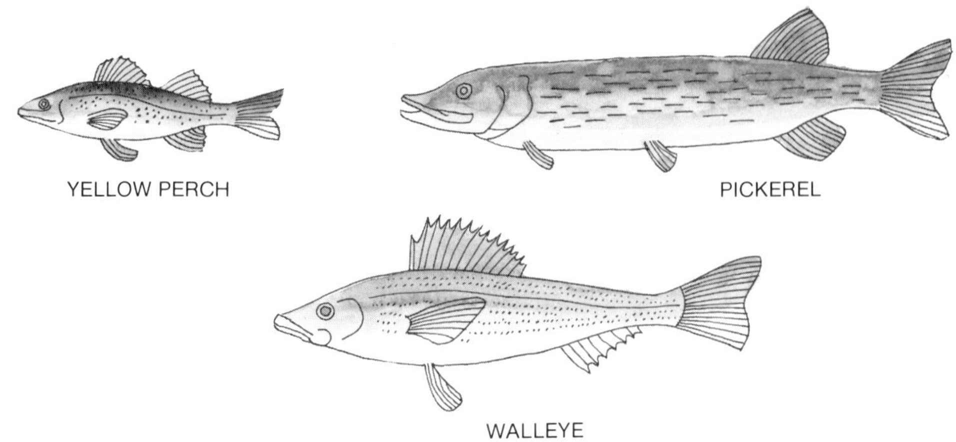

I discovered how exciting northern pike can be one day while lazily fishing for panfish on a lake. I'd bait the hook and send it sailing out to the water, and then I'd watch for the bobber to begin nodding in the water. When a little panfish pulled the bobber under, I'd snatch the fish in.

Suddenly, my bobber plunged beneath the water and kept on going down. I snatched back in alarm and a huge submarine of a fish shot to the surface, jumping and spraying water to the bank where I stood. It seemed to be as long as I was.

Then the big pike coughed up a little panfish, which had eaten my worm just before being eaten by the big fish.

"Big fish eat little fish," said an old fisherman standing nearby. He was right!

COLDWATER FISH

Sometimes you find coldwater fish living in ponds and lakes along with the panfish we've described. Coldwater fish also live in streams, lakes, and rivers that remain cool through the summer. Brook trout, rainbow trout, brown trout, and cutthroat trout are fish that need cold water to survive, as do Atlantic salmon and Pacific salmon—fish that are born in fresh water and swim to the ocean to grow before returning to lay eggs for another generation of fish. These fish are called *anadromous,* a Greek word meaning "running upward."

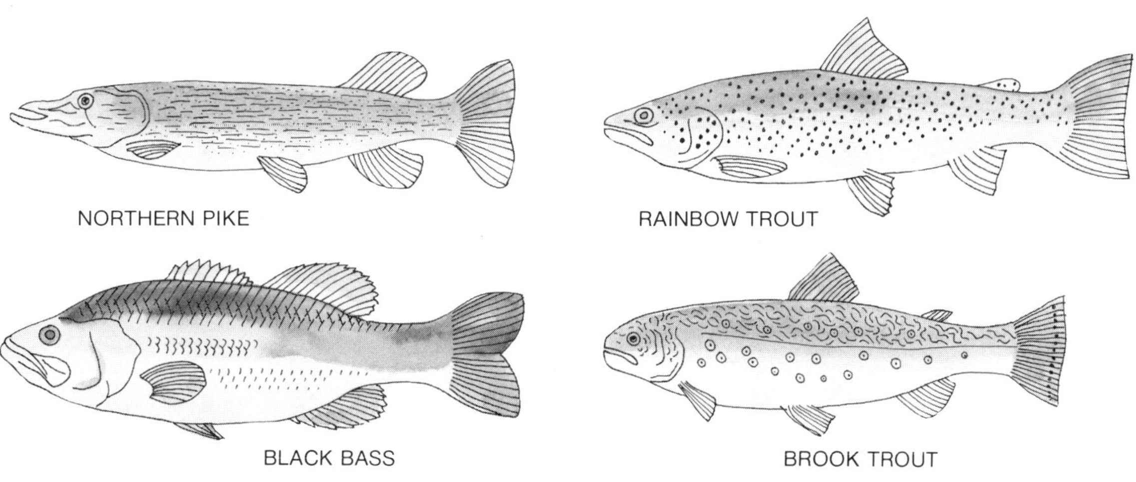

NORTHERN PIKE

RAINBOW TROUT

BLACK BASS

BROOK TROUT

Trout live in fine places—small creeks fed by cold spring waters, big brawling rivers, and tiny brooks choked by alders. It can be challenging to catch trout, and it's worth the effort.

When I was a boy I knew of a big trout that lived in a river near my home. I would lie on the riverbank and watch the big fish come out to feed just before dark each evening. Try as I might, however, I could not catch the trout.

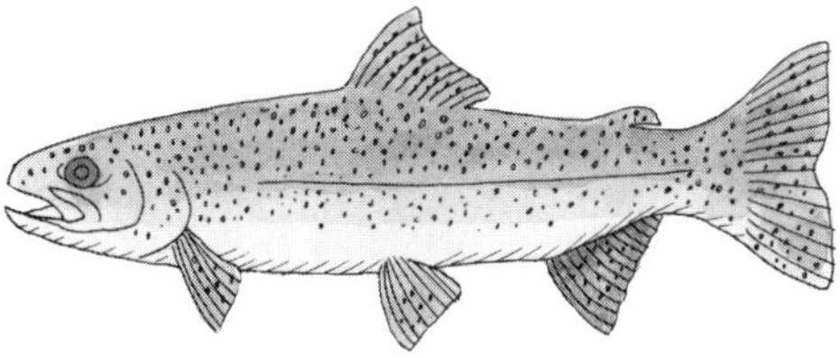

LAKE TROUT

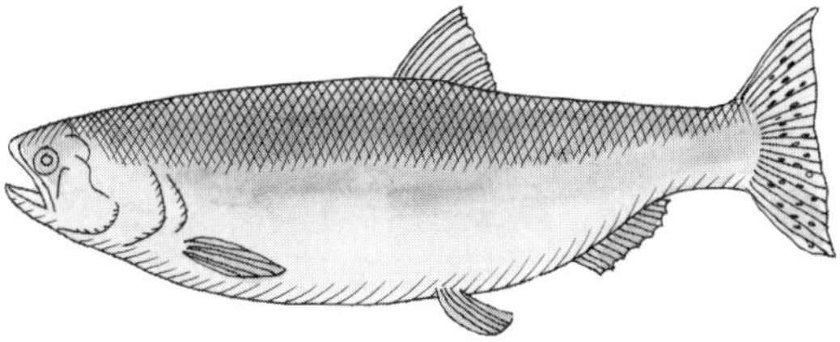

COHO SALMON

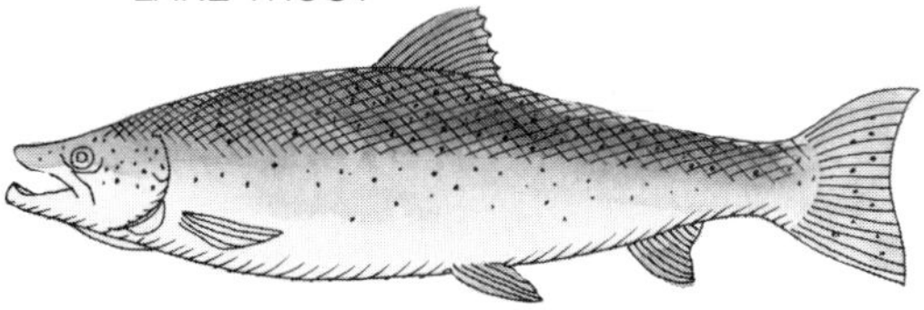

ATLANTIC SALMON

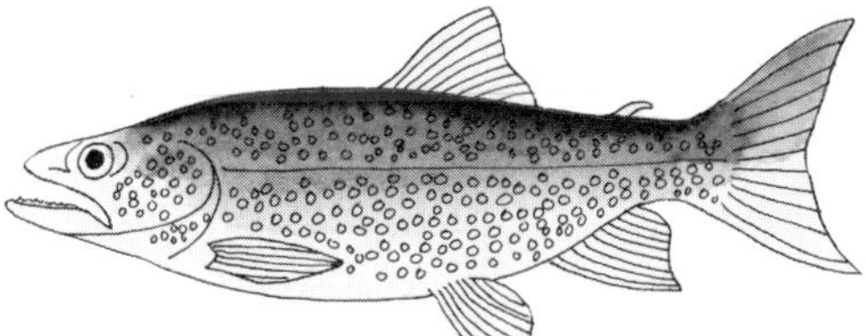

BROWN TROUT

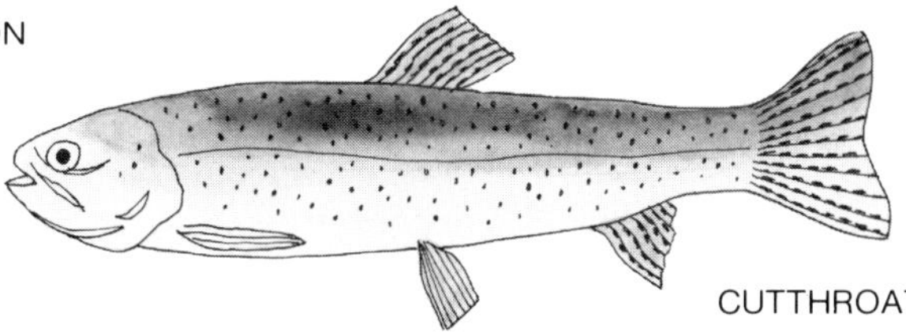

CUTTHROAT TROUT

Sometimes northern pike can be nearly as large as the fisherman. This one was 16 pounds.

One day, when the river was high and muddy, I tossed a hook baited with worms into the wise old trout's favorite feeding spot and let it sink and drift down in the current until it reached bottom.

When my line suddenly stopped, I lifted the rod, and a great weight throbbed along the line. With a splash a huge fish burst to the surface, the sun shining on its yellow sides and water spraying from its shaking head. Realizing it was hooked, the big fish rushed from the pool and headed down the river. It took all my line until I saw the bare reel spool. The line snapped and my fish was gone. I stood with my heart pounding. Then I ran home to tell the story of the big fish that got away.

SALTWATER FISH

There can be just as many exciting experiences for you fishing on the beaches and jetties by the oceans. Wherever you walk along the sea—on docks, rock walls, or along the dunes of summer beaches—you are near fish.

These saltwater fish are stronger than freshwater fish. Saltwater fish are almost too numerous to list, but here are a few you will find when you begin fishing.

Inshore Fish

Inshore saltwater fish live along the beaches and around docks and jetties. They include striped bass, bluefish, skup, flounder, sea trout, drum, sea perch, bonefish, ladyfish, snapper, barracuda, tarpon, and many small fish.

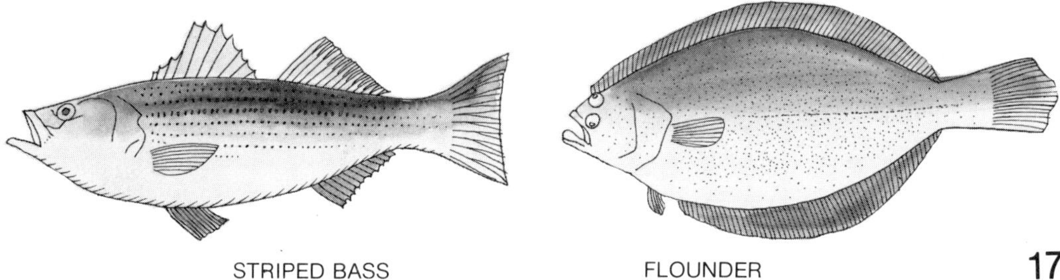

STRIPED BASS   FLOUNDER

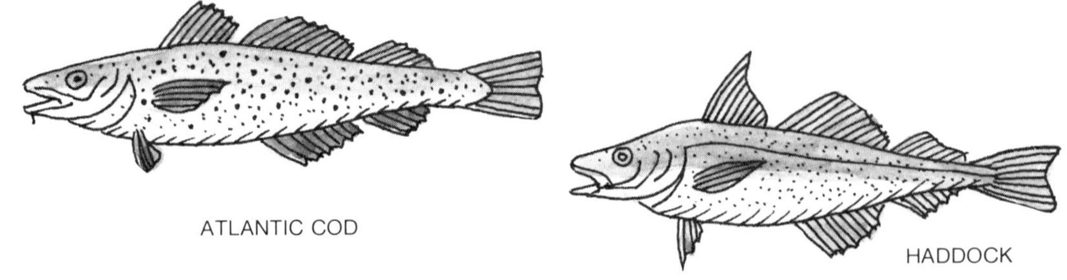

Offshore Fish

Offshore ocean fishing requires a strong boat for a safe journey to and from the fishing grounds, for out where the water is very deep the fish are very large. Mammoth black and blue marlin cruise the deeps and leap skyward when hooked behind a boat. Wahoo, king mackerel, dolphin, bluefin tuna (some of them over a thousand pounds!) and small tuna, albacore, false albacore, and bright silver sailfish challenge the ocean-going fishermen.

Other ocean fishermen reach their fishing spot on drift boats equipped to take fifty or more fishermen for bottom fishing. You can leave right from New York City on a drift boat that has all the equipment you'll need for cod, haddock, and other species.

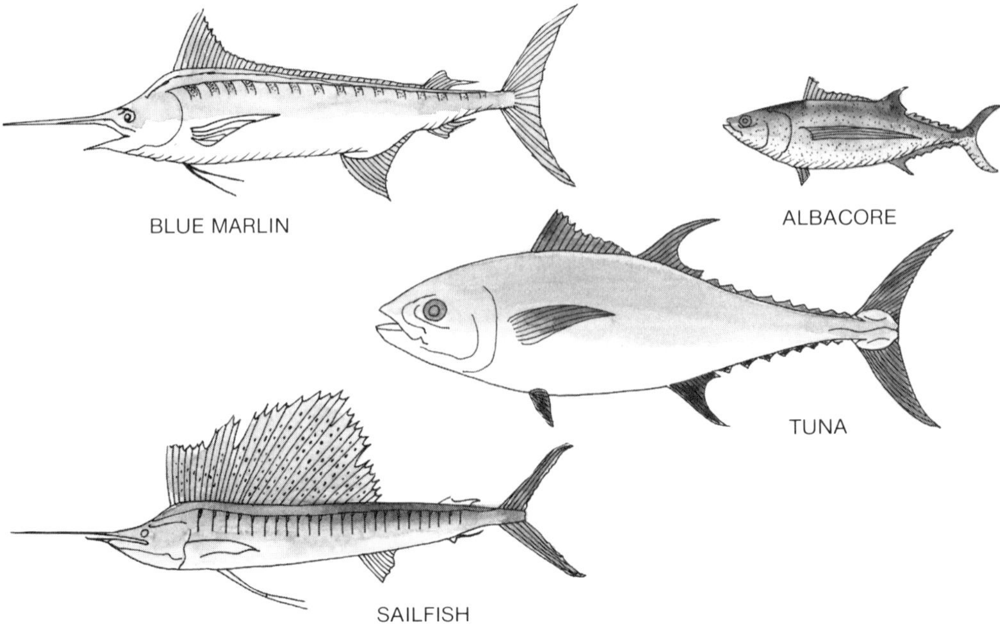

18

3

THE DIFFERENT TYPES OF FISHING

There are five places to fish. And where you fish usually determines *how* you fish. The places to fish are in streams, lakes, ponds, and oceans—inshore and offshore.

In casting a drop line,
the fisherman uses no pole.

Photo by *The Record, Hackensack, N.J.*

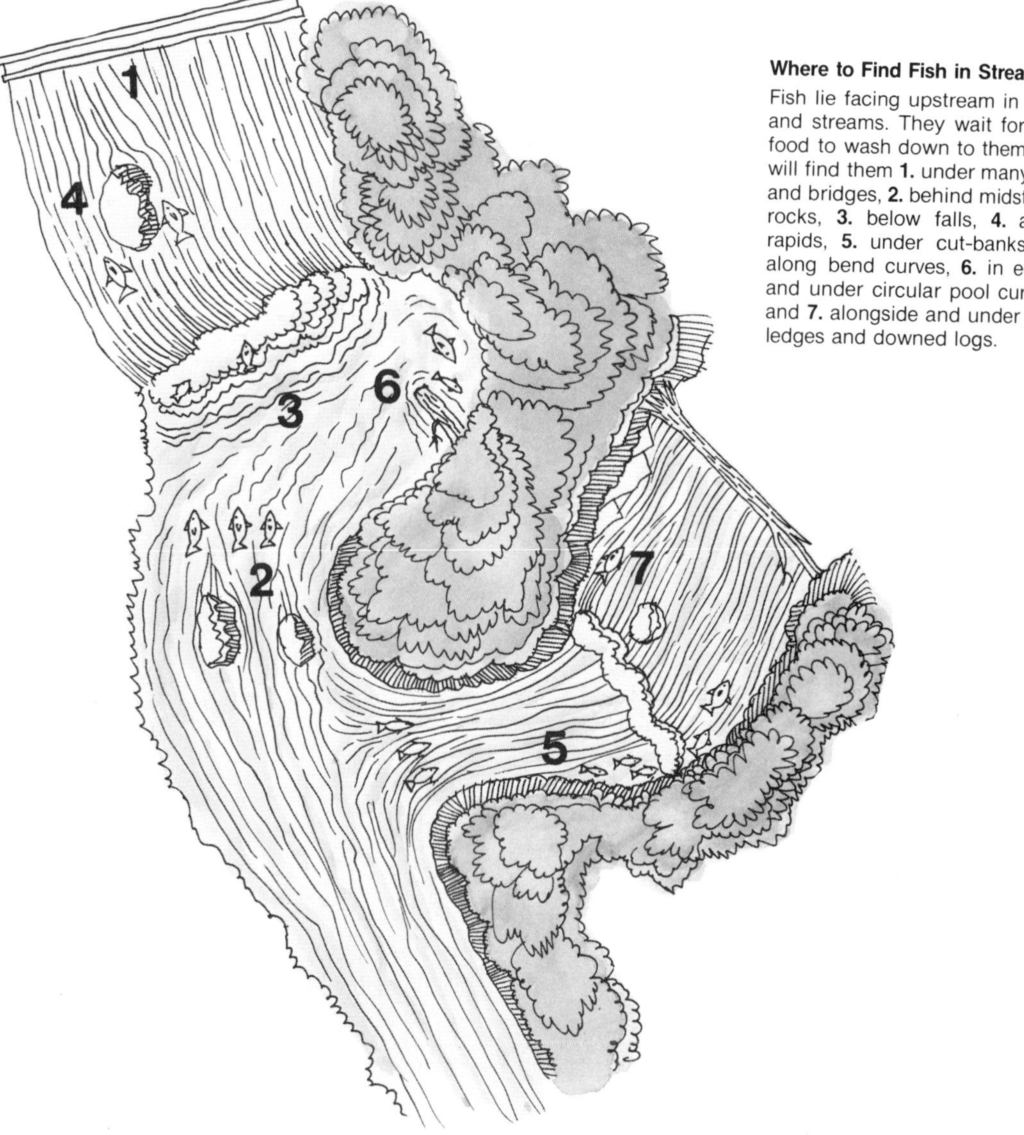

Where to Find Fish in Streams
Fish lie facing upstream in rivers and streams. They wait for their food to wash down to them. You will find them **1.** under many logs and bridges, **2.** behind midstream rocks, **3.** below falls, **4.** above rapids, **5.** under cut-banks and along bend curves, **6.** in eddies and under circular pool currents and **7.** alongside and under bank ledges and downed logs.

Stream Fishing

Fish that live in streams usually lie facing upstream, waiting for their food to wash down to them. Since the water is moving, the fish lie where it will not wash them away. They hide under currents, beside rocks, and under fallen trees and streamside banks. To fish for them we must throw a bait of lure where they can see it. Often we must wade in the water to reach the fish.

Pond and Lake Fishing

The fish in ponds and lakes must swim to find their food because there is no current to bring the food to them. These fish we can reach from shore by casting our bait out, or we can go out to fish in boats. In either case, we must know where the fish are to fish for them.

Where to Fish in Lakes and Ponds

You will find fish lying in predictable places in lakes and ponds. They are **1.** boat docks, **2.** outlets, **3.** shoreline ledges, **4.** rocks, **5.** inlets to the lake or pond, **6.** along weed beds, **7.** by logs and leaning trees and **8.** in deep holes.

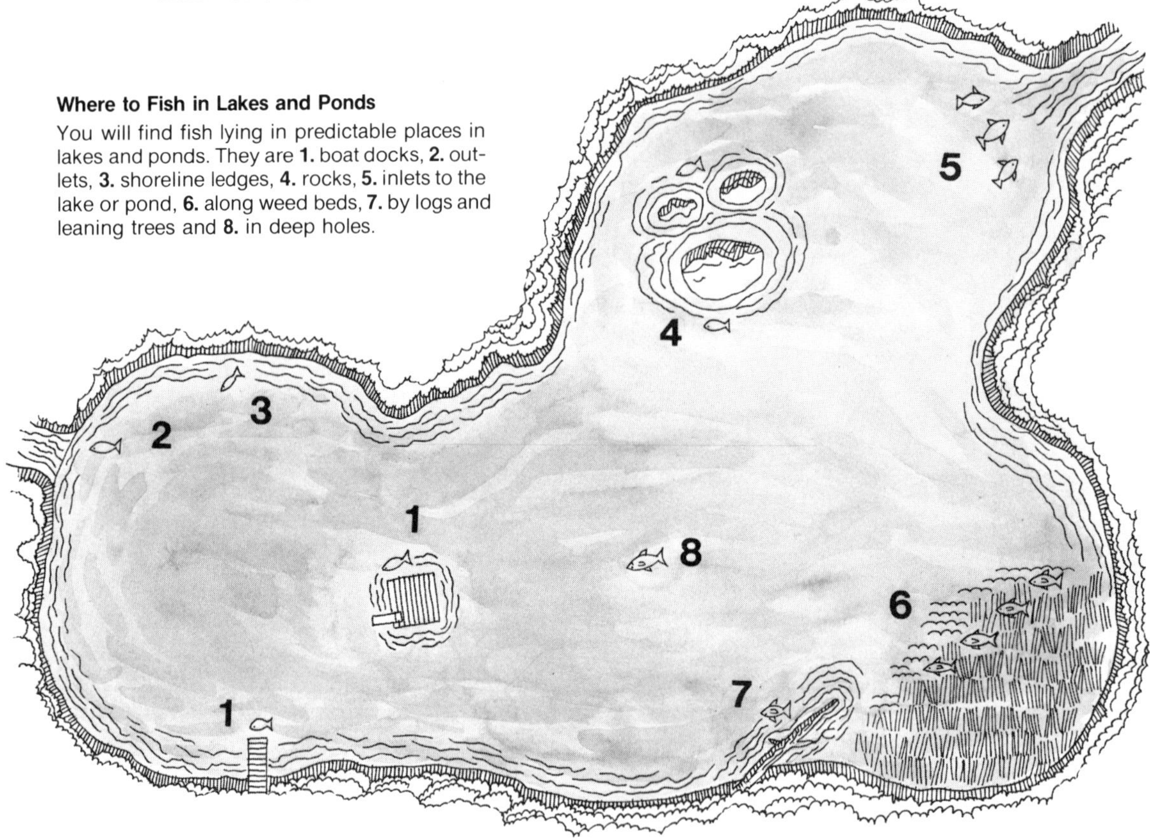

Lake and pond fish lie at the inlets and outlets. They also lie around rock piles, jetties, boat docks, weed beds, and logs; and they like to swim along the shorelines looking for food. Sometimes we can spot them breaking the water surface with their backs as they swim and feed on insects. Learn to be observant: Spotting fish is the first step in fishing.

Ocean Fishing — Inshore

Inshore fish often move with the change of seasons and with changes of the tide each day. An experienced saltwater fisherman can teach you how to "read the tides"—learn how the fish move and feed with changes of the tide each day. If you live near the ocean, you can find the tide tables in your local newspaper. And saltwater fishermen can tell you which species of fish the seasons bring. Learning tides and seasonal fish movements is essential to inshore fishing.

Ocean Fishing — Offshore

Far from shore the big game fish of the oceans follow the schools of bait fish on which they feed. Often these big fish swim thousands of miles in their travels along such currents as the Gulf Stream and the Japan Current. To reach the offshore fish, fishermen use large, expensive boats and the most modern fishing equipment.

Offshore fish are usually very large. They are considered trophies by the fishermen, who display them proudly back at the boat dock.

Five Methods of Fishing

The five methods of fishing are

1. still-fishing
2. fly-fishing
3. bait-fishing
4. spin-fishing
5. trolling

When *still-fishing*, you sit or stand and allow your bait to rest quietly in the water. Often you use a long cane pole with a hook, bobber, and bait. Still-fishermen usually fish in lakes, ponds, and slow-moving rivers. They wait for the fish to come to their baits, and they watch their bobbers for the bite of a fish.

You can still-fish from a stream bank or lake or pond shoreline during daylight or at night. You can stand, sit or simply use a forked stick to rest your rod. A good way to begin is with a hook, worm, bobber and line attached to your spin-casting or bait rod. Adjust your line and bobber so the bait is just off bottom and watch the bobber for a tug. Keep your line just tight enough to pull up when the bobber goes under to "strike" the fish and set the hook in its jaw. Small fish will cause the bobber to bob up and down. Big fish will take it right under the water.

Fly-fishermen attempt to match fish foods with "flies"—bits of feathers and tinsel tied to hooks. The flies imitate insects, minnows, and other things fish like to eat. Fly-fishermen fish their flies on the surface, dry-fly fishing, and underneath the water, wet-fly fishing. They use special "fly lines" for their fishing.

Bait fishermen use bait rods and reels for fishing; usually for bass, inshore ocean trolling, and for lake "downrigger" fishing.

Spin-fishing is the most widely used method of fishing. Spin rods and reels are used in both freshwater and saltwater fishing—in streams, lakes, ponds, and inshore and offshore.

Troll fishermen drag their lines and baits behind a boat. Often they use motors to drive their boats, and modern troll fishermen use "downriggers"—rod, wheel, and cable devices mounted on the boat which take baits deep into lakes, ponds, and ocean waters.

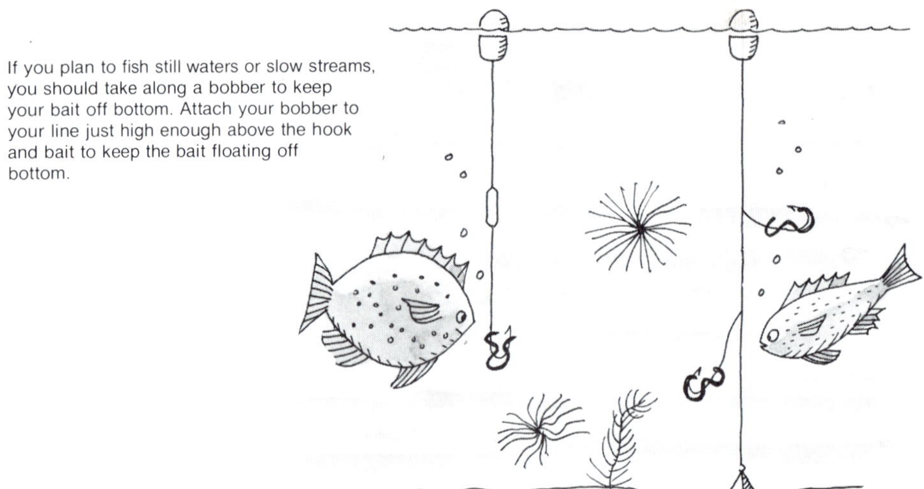

If you plan to fish still waters or slow streams, you should take along a bobber to keep your bait off bottom. Attach your bobber to your line just high enough above the hook and bait to keep the bait floating off bottom.

4

BASIC EQUIPMENT YOU WILL NEED

Tackle for Stream, Pond, and Lake Fishing

You will need a close-faced or open-faced spinning reel equipped with a 6- or 8-pound-test monofilament line, bait box, sinkers, hooks (#4 to #6), rubber boots, fish net, spinning lures, a creel in which to carry your fish, and a small knife to clean your catch. Complete spinning outfits can be purchased in fishing-tackle stores and in most large chain stores. Prices begin around $20. You can begin your stream fishing for about $25.

You'll also need bait to begin fishing streams. Most young fishermen begin with worms and nightcrawlers they capture themselves, or they buy them for about $1 a dozen.

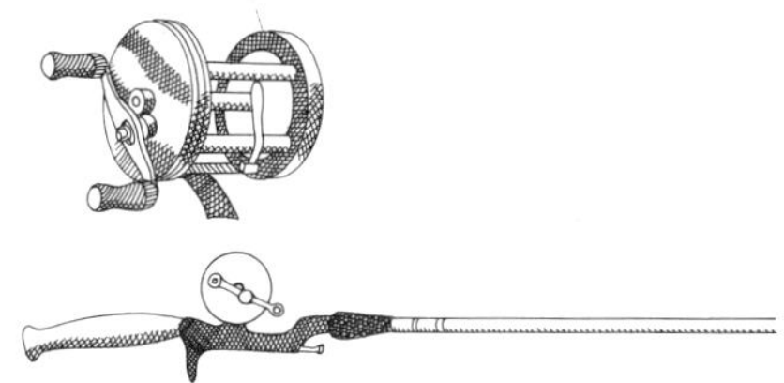

OPEN-FACED SPINNING REEL: Open-faced reels have line wound on a reel spool. The line runs off the reel and up through the rod guides to the lure or bait. The weight of the lure or bait pulls the line off the reel spool when the rod and lure are cast.

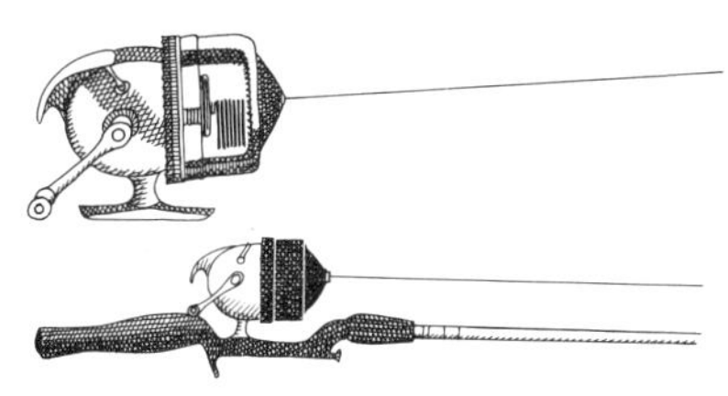

CLOSE-FACED SPINNING REEL: The line is wound on the reel spool inside the reel and is completely covered. Close-faced reels are inexpensive — starting at around $8 — and easy to use for the beginner.

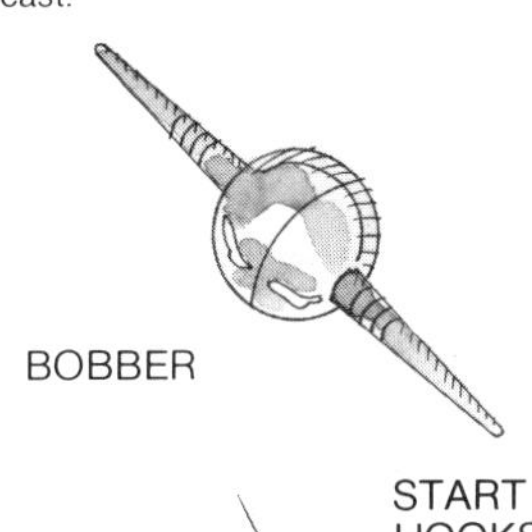

BOBBER

OPEN-FACED (OR CLOSE-FACED) SPINNING REEL, ROD AND 6- or 8 POUND TEST MONOFILAMENT LINE.

START WITH #6 OR #8 HOOKS. THEY ARE SAFE WHEN STUCK TO A CORK.

BAIT-CASTING REEL AND ROD

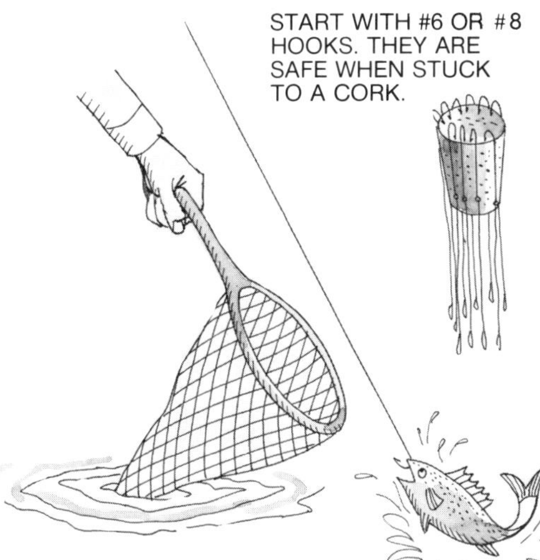

SMALL NET

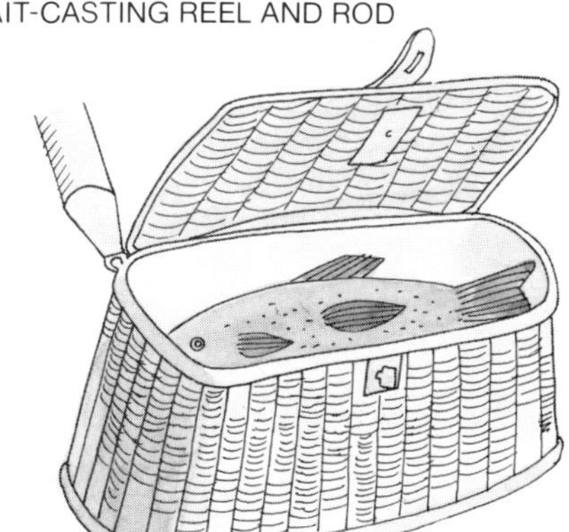

CREEL

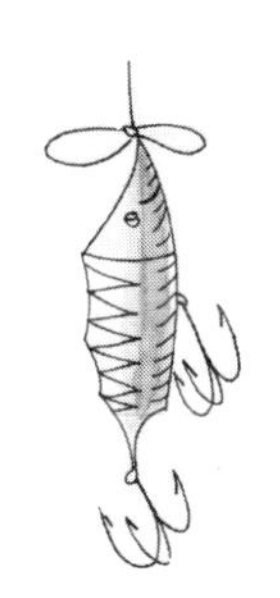

SPINNING LURES

HIP-WADER BOOTS

SPOOL OF LINE

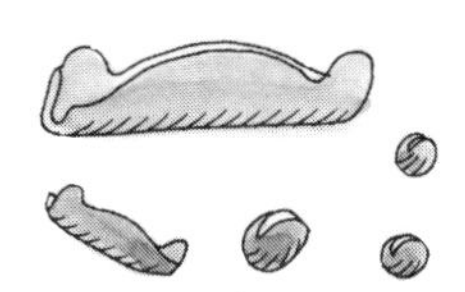

SINKERS

SCALER AND JACKNIFE

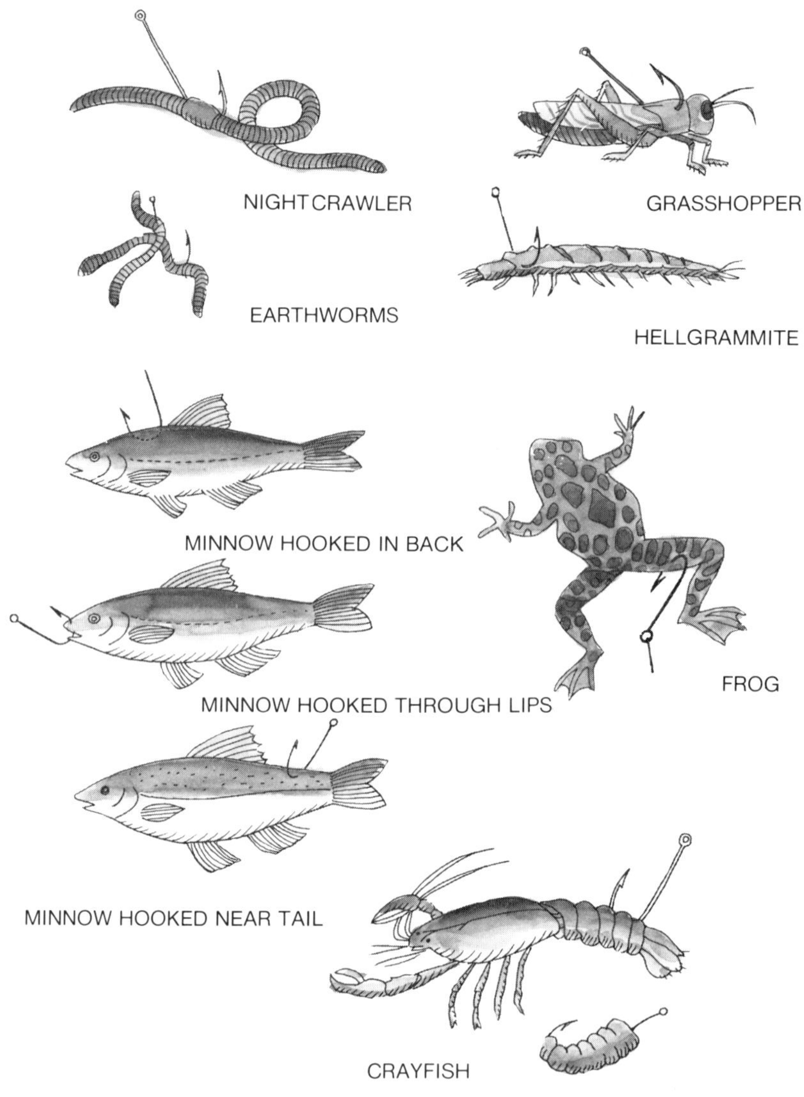

You can dig worms in your back yard or garden. Night-crawlers come out on damp spring and summer nights. The best places to find them are lawns, golf courses, and in grassy parks. To capture them walk along slowly with a flashlight trained on the ground; creep up and pounce on the crawlers before they can crawl underground. Don't stretch them; they keep better un-stretched. Keep crawlers and worms in cool places—a refrigerator or damp cellar. Never leave them in the sun.

The same fishing gear will work well for pond and lake fishing. Add several bobbers to your tackle and add a tackle box to keep lures, hooks, and other tackle in. A "stringer" made of light rope can be strung through the gills of your large lake fish to keep them alive and fresh until you clean them.

When your rod, reel, line, sinker, hook and bait are put together properly you are ready to fish.

Small boats such as canoes and rowboats are used to fish small lakes and ponds. However, never go out without oars or paddles and life vests.

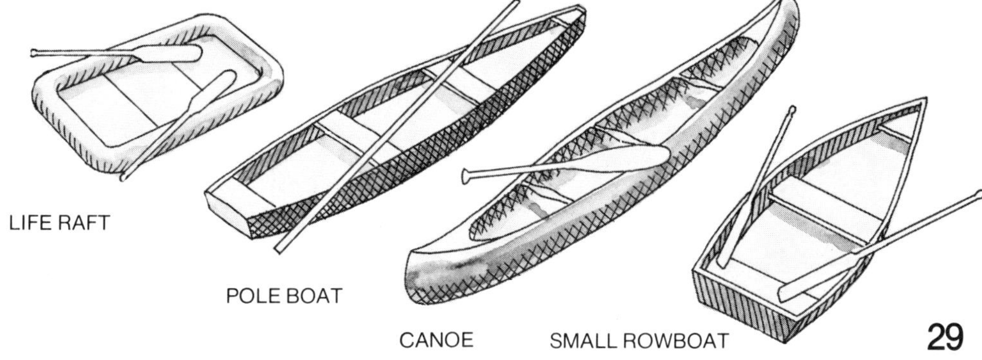

On large lakes you will need a large boat equipped with everything called for by Coast Guard regulations—lights, life vests, etc. Some lake fishermen use trolling equipment—downriggers, bait rods and reels, deep-running lures and flies, and special "rigs" to make them work properly. For this fishing you'll need advice from the manager of a boat marina that specializes in lake fishing.

Tackle for Inshore Ocean Fishing

You'll need larger rods and reels for saltwater fishing than for freshwater fishing, because the fish are larger and stronger. Large spinning rods and reels are the universal favorites because they are easy to use and care for. A good rod and reel can be purchased for around $135. Inexpensive secondhand rods and reels are available, but be sure the reel is working properly. Saltwater tackle must be washed after using or the salt will quickly cause corrosion.

Stainless steel hooks are a good investment. Steel hooks corrode quickly in salt water. Your inshore hooks should be from size #6 for small fish to 5/0 or larger for big fish such as striped bass. You'll need a large boat net for the large fish and, in some cases, a gaff. Large sinkers are very important for your shore and jetty fishing. They're inexpensive, but you'll lose them in the bottom rocks, so buy more than you think you'll need. Other tackle to include would be a stainless steel knife for fish cleaning, ice chest for keeping fish cool, and a fish scaler for scaling fish. Get advice on baits from a bait-and-tackle-store proprietor who can tell you the baits the fish are feeding on—sea worms, clams, etc.—and who can also advise you on your tackle.

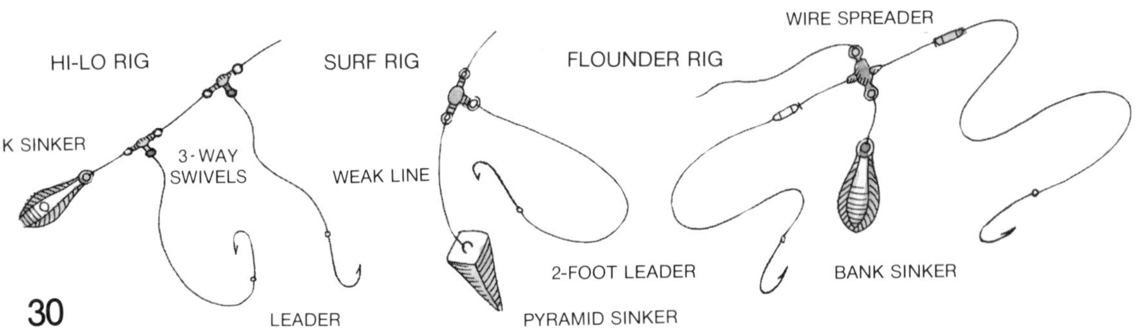

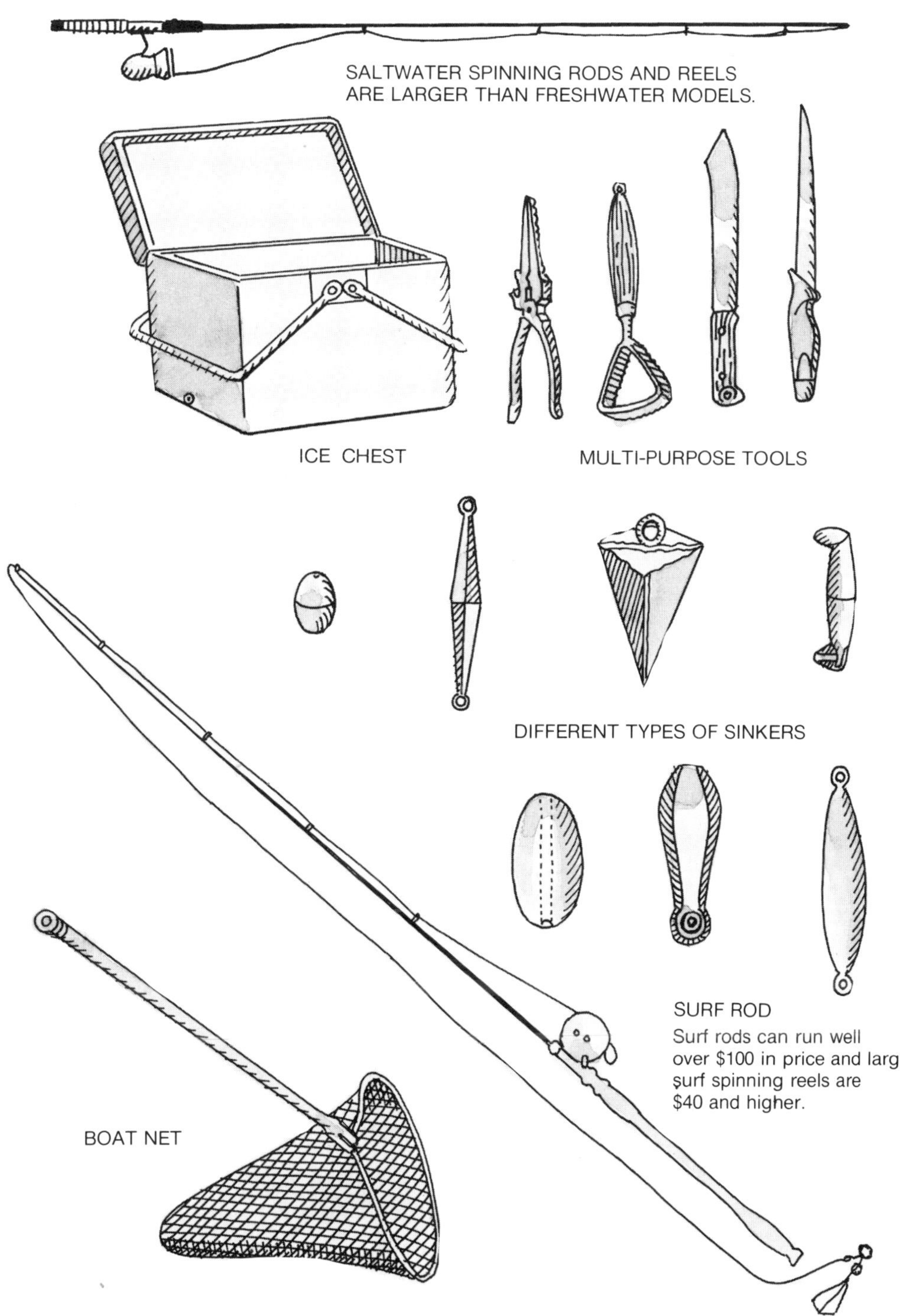

SURF ROD

Surf rods can run well over $100 in price and large surf spinning reels are $40 and higher.

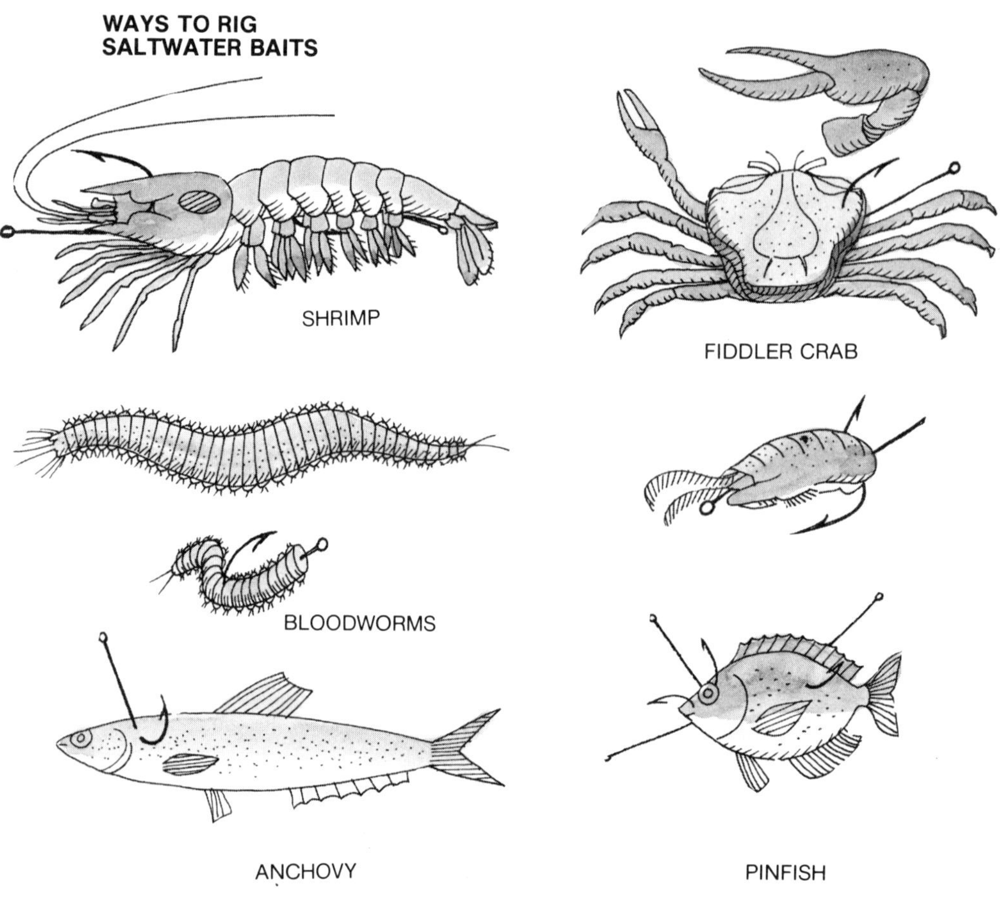

Tackle for Offshore Ocean Fishing

Offshore tackle is usually provided by the boat charter, but some fishermen equip themselves with very large rods and stainless steel reels with heavy lines. The boats are equipped with fighting chairs and harnesses to hold the fishermen in place while fighting fish.

Ocean-going drift boats also provide fishermen with rods, reels, lines, and bait; but you'll need to bring your lunch, sunglasses, seasick pills, rain gear, and a warm sweater. An ice chest for your fish, cleaning knife, tackle box to hold hooks and other fishing gear, and a small gaff round out your tackle.

5

LET'S GO FISHING

Let's Fish in the Pond

We're going fishing today on Spring Lake in the city park. But before we do, we need a fishing license and a copy of the fishing laws from our town office or city hall. Next we need to equip ourselves for the fishing. What should we take?

Spring Lake is really a small pond. It has a shallow bottom and many panfish. Since we will fish from shore, we need no boat or life jackets; but we do need bait (we've decided on worms today) and a bait box in which to keep them fresh and cool. (A coffee can with damp leaves and coffee grounds will hold the worms.) We could have used other baits as well—grasshoppers, crickets, and other small things that live around the lake.

For our tackle we can use either a drop line or a spinning rod, light line, and reel. We'll also need a bobber, hooks, sinkers, and a creel in which to carry our fish. We need a small knife to clean the fish, and we may need calf-length rubber boots if the shoreline is wet. Before we begin fishing, we run our monofilament line off the reel, up through the fishing rod guides; and to the line end we tie a hook with an "improved clinch knot." To the

line we attach a bobber about two feet above the hook. We thread our worm on the hook and we are ready to fish.

Where to begin fishing? Let's take a look at the fishing diagram in Chapter 3 to see where the fish should be. Panfish like to swim in "schools" around boat docks, weed beds, sunken logs, and along shorelines. Large warmwater fish—black bass, pickerel, and pike—like to hide under logs and trees; and they too like weed beds and rock piles.

We'll fish these places by walking the shorelines, keeping our eyes open for dimples and rings on the lake's surface where schools of fish are moving and feeding. When we spot a school, we'll cast our bait to the fish. The panfish will bite the worm and tug the bobber under, and we will catch one fish after another.

Let's Fish in the Stream

If we tire of lake fishing we can try the stream that flows out of it. But first let's consider how deep the stream water is. Do we know how to swim? If we fall in we might be swept away by the current. Let's make a rule: No boat fishing without a life vest, and no stream fishing without first learning how to swim and then being accompanied by someone.

Now that we're at the stream, let's think about where the fish are. The diagram in Chapter 3 tells us stream fish lie on the bottom, below the current. They look up to spot their food drifting overhead. They lie behind rocks, in current eddies, and at the outflow and inflow of the lake.

Because of the current's swift flow, we'll have to put lead sinkers on the line to sink the hooks and worms down to where the fish are. We'll cast out and let the bait sink and drift along the bottom to the fish. When we feel the fish bite and tug on the bait, we'll tighten the line by lifting the rod tip to "set the hook" in the fish's jaw. Then we'll let the fish fight against the tension of the line and rod until it tires. When the fish is tired, we'll crank him in with our fishing reel.

Here on the stream we've used the same spinning rod and reel we used on the lake, but we need to know more about casting here because we must cast to tight protected spots where the fish lie, often far from where we stand. We also need higher boots than we needed along the lake bank, because at times we must wade into the stream to get closer to the fish.

In the stream the water is colder than it was in the lake. We're fishing for coldwater fish—trout, instead of the sunfish and perch that we found in the lake. We'll need a net to "land" the fish, and we need a bait box we can attach to our belt so we can carry our worms with us into the stream.

When we wade we go carefully, because we could slip and be swept away by the current. We try to wade quietly, because the fish can hear underwater sounds made by our feet. We also try to keep our shadow off the water and our profile low, because the fish can spot us as we approach. We work our way downstream as we fish, but sometimes we fish upstream and cast ahead, letting the bait drift back down to us.

Let's Fish in the Lake

This day we will go fishing on the big lake—Lake Michigan. It's still-water fishing out there, but there's a difference. The lake is so vast that we need a boat to reach all the fishing. Today we'll charter a boat that has all the equipment for fishing salmon, lake trout, and other coldwater fish. Our boat is a 30-footer equipped with sonar (called a "fish-finder") and special rods to get our baits and lures down to the fish. These "downriggers" are a short rod and pulley wheel equipped with wire line and a lead ball to take our lures down to 80 feet or deeper. We'll be "trolling" today, with the boat moving to make our lures swim through the water like bait fish the salmon and lake trout feed on.

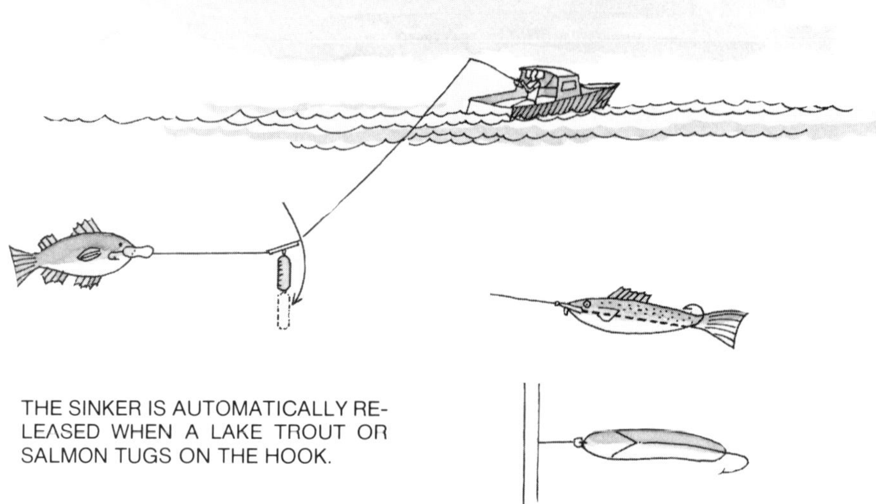

Since the captain has all the rods and reels we'll need, we won't have to bring our own rods. We are also equipped with life vests in case of rough weather, but we'll need to bring along suntan lotion to protect us against sunburn, and we'll need rain gear in case of squalls.

The rods the boat captain attaches to the downriggers are bait-casting rods and reels. He drops the lures and bait to the bottom, where he usually finds lake trout; then he cruises along, letting the lures troll and hoping a lake trout will spot one, give chase, and bite.

There! A fish has grabbed the lure and released the line from the downrigger! Grab the rod! Let the fish run and pull the line from the reel until it's tired. Now reel the fish in. Let it run again if it wants. Don't try to fight the fish too fast! I'll net the fish as you reel it alongside the boat. He's ours! A nice 12-pounder!

Let's try spin-casting on the lake surface while we rig for trolling again. Cast a spinner out there; you might catch a coho salmon cruising on the surface for bait fish. Cast as far as you can, then reel in just fast enough to make the spinner blade work.

There! The fish has hooked himself. Let him run. Set your "drag" a little tighter, but not too tight or he'll break the line. Now you have him beat. Reel in so I can net him. A fine 10-pound coho salmon!

Let's Fish in the Ocean Bay

Let's go down to the dock of the bay today and hand-line for skup, school bass, small stripers, and rock codfish. We'll fish from the jetties and the dock, walking and throwing our baited hook weighted with sinkers. We'll buy a small box of clams to cut, bait the hook, and throw out. As the hook sinks to the bottom, we'll retrieve it slowly until we feel a tug. Then we'll "set the hook" and fight the fish in.

Or we can take our spinning rods and reels and cast lures to the bay while we walk along the shoreline. We'll reel the lures in after we cast so they spin and swim like natural fish in the water. When we get a "strike" from a fish we'll strike back by raising the rod tip. The fight will be on!

We can also fish the channel at the mouth of the bay and catch flounder in the slow water where the bottom is soft. Or we can walk along the beach and cast out to the surf for stripers. We'll have to use heavier line, though, and we'll have to stay out at night, when the striped bass swim in to feed along the shoreline. We'll need surf-casting rods for this fishing, and we'll first learn to rig big sinkers and special baits for the fishing. We'll also have to practice casting the heavy "rigs" out beyond the breakers of the surf. Stripers are big fish, so we'll dig in our heels and lean back into the rod to fight the fish. We'll learn how to set the reel drag properly and how to drag the big fish out of the surf without being swept away by the beach undertow. We'll fish with experienced fishermen to learn all the tricks.

THE SURF FISHERMAN MUST CAST FAR OUT WITH HEAVILY WEIGHTED RIGS.

Better yet, let's go boat-fishing in the bay and troll for bluefish on the surface. Or we can rig deep-running lures to get down to where the stripers lie. If the bluefish are in season, we can cast plastic plugs to big schools of them, and the fish will hit as fast as we can throw. We'll be so tired from fighting fish that we will have to head home.

We can use either spinning rods or bait rods and reels for the bluefish, which will be in the bays feeding on bait fish called "bunker." We'll need floating lures that are large and brightly colored. We'll also need suntan lotion, a large boat net, an ice chest to keep the fish fresh until we get home, and warm clothing and rain gear to protect against the ocean chill and spray. We'll use "snap swivels" for attaching our lures to our heavy monofilament and "wire leaders"—or the sharp bluefish teeth might break our lines.

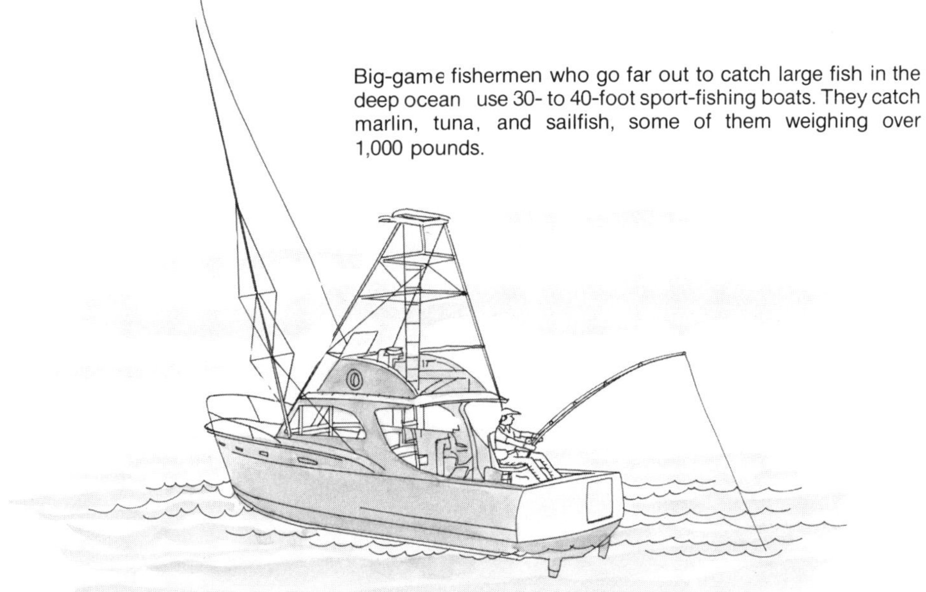

Big-game fishermen who go far out to catch large fish in the deep ocean use 30- to 40-foot sport-fishing boats. They catch marlin, tuna, and sailfish, some of them weighing over 1,000 pounds.

Let's Fish in the Ocean

If it's a nice day, let's go out on a party boat for codfish, haddock, and mackerel. We'll leave New York harbor before dawn, and we'll have all our equipment provided for us by the boat. We'll steam several hours out to sea and then drift and fish, dropping our lines overboard to the bottom where the cod lie. We'll fish with cut bait, and we'll catch enough fish for several meals. We'll take along our own lunches, sunglasses, rain gear, and seasick pills, just in case. Our tackle box will hold extra hooks and sinkers and a stainless steel knife for cutting and cleaning fish. We'll be out at sea all day, and our ice chest will be full when we return.

6

CASTING AND
HOW TO DO IT

If you can throw a ball, you can cast with a fishing rod. The motion of your arm is the same in most cases.

In casting with a spinning rod, you are actually using the rod to throw a small weight at the end of the line. When you throw the weight, it pulls the line from the spinning reel and line and lure-fly to the spot where you aim the rod.

You cast with your wrist and arm, as though you were going to throw a ball. Where you point the rod tip is where the lure or bait will go. Aim high and the lure will sail high; low and the lure will fall near you; right—lure goes right; left—lure goes left.

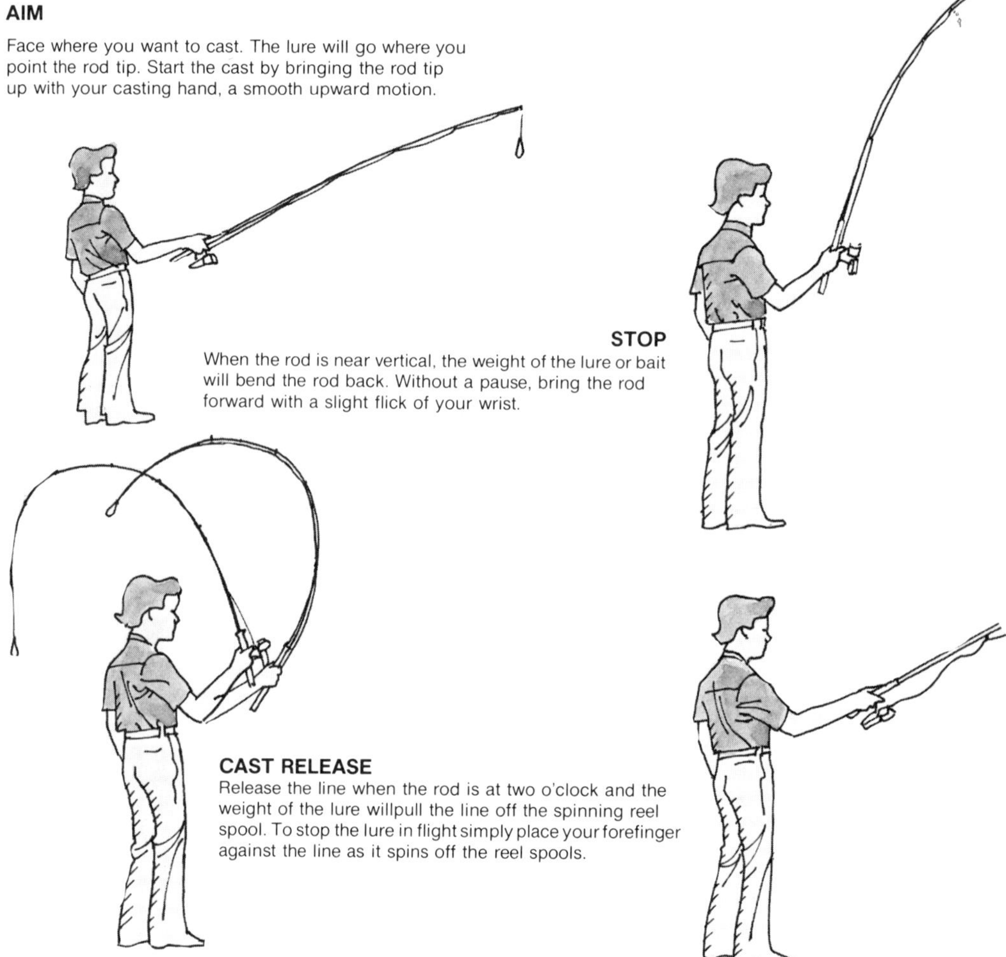

Learning to use the flex of the rod to cast the lure is the key to good spin-casting. Practice is the key to casting. Ten minutes of casting a lure (with the hooks taken off) in your back yard should make you a proficient caster. Your practice should also give you a feel for throwing the bail over on the top of your open-faced spinning reel, and it should give you a sense of timing in releasing the line held in your right or left index finger, depending on whether you are right- or left-handed.

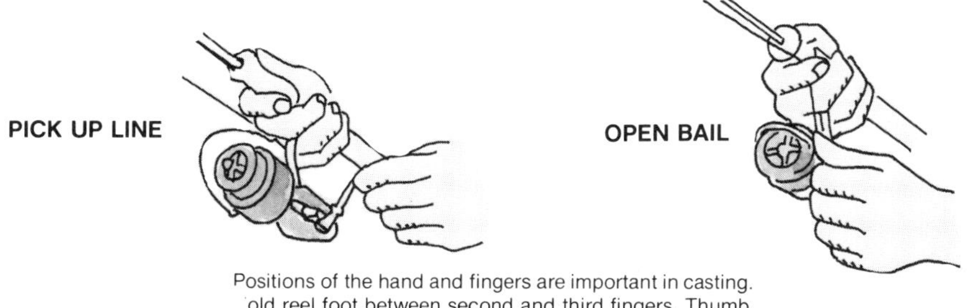

Positions of the hand and fingers are important in casting. old reel foot between second and third fingers. Thumb top of rod grip. Disengage reel bail with left hand. Hold with extended index finger.

With index finger hold line free of spool before casting. Use index finger while casting to slow lure and line speed of reel spool. Stop cast with index finger by pressing line as it uncoils.

Close-faced reels are cast by depressing a button on the reel at just the right moment during the casting motion. Good casting only requires practice to acquire the timing.

Accuracy in casting can make the difference in catching or not catching fish. Practice your accuracy by casting a lure to target spots on your lawn.

7
FINDING OUT MORE ABOUT FISHING

Now that we've led you to the water and taught you how to fish, you're probably wondering what lies ahead for you as a fisherman. You may be asking yourself how you can find more information about the kind of fishing you like most. After all, if you live near salt water the chances are that saltwater fishing will be your favorite pastime; but if you live near fresh water, the ponds, lakes, and streams are where you'll fish most often.

The place to learn fishing is with one of your relatives, if possible. A relative can teach you the tricks of fishing technique that will work where you choose to fish. Remember that for each type of fishing there is a technique that is different from that used in other types of fishing. You could spend the rest of your life learning fishing techniques used on fresh and salt waters, but you could not learn them all. There are too many.

Begin by choosing the fishing you enjoy most. Then begin to learn that fishing technique by searching outdoor magazines, such as *Outdoor Life, Sports Afield, Field and Stream, Fly Fisherman,* and others you will find on your newsstand. You'll quickly find that by browsing through these magazines you can discover

stories that specialize in, for instance, bass fishing in ponds and lakes, downrigger fishing for lake trout and salmon, saltwater fishing for bluefish and other species. When you find a story that deals with your favorite fishing, buy the magazine.

Another source of fishing knowledge is the Boy Scouts of America, an organization that offers a merit badge in fishing and the instruction reading to achieve the badge. Hunting and fishing clubs in your area can also be a source of information and training in fishing, especially if you ask older members for their help. Fishing-tackle stores near good fishing spots in saltwater or fresh-water fishing areas are an excellent source of information on how to fish and where to fish. Most fishing-tackle-store managers will tell you what to buy for any kind of fishing you want to do. And most store managers will also tell you how to rig reels, rods, lines, and lures or baits for fishing.

Books are perhaps your best source of thorough information on all types of fishing. We cannot list all the fishing books in print here, for there are too many, but your library should have many books on fishing. The library is a good place to begin your research. You will also find lists of books on both hunting and fishing in the outdoor magazines we've listed. Some of the magazines have book clubs which offer fishing books at special prices for members. If you join an outdoor book club you will receive notices of all the new books offered by the club.

These are some of the ways you can find more information on fishing, but in the end the best way to learn to fish is to do it. Fish as often as you can and wherever you can. Very soon you will learn to hunt fish, and you will learn how to catch them when you've found them. Fishing requires effort to achieve, just as any other endeavor in life. The fisherman who gets up early and fishes hard usually catches the most fish and has the most fun.

In order to have enough fish left in our streams, lakes, and ponds to fish another day and to provide fishing for others, let's resolve to release all the fish we don't intend to eat. Let's resolve also that we will work for clean waters where fish can survive, for without "habitat"—waters that are right for fish—we cannot have these exciting forms of wildlife.

There is no end to the challenges of fishing. As you learn and become a veteran in your experiences, you may move on to the highest fishing challenges of all: fly-fishing and all its disciplines, fly-tying, rod-building, and the many stream techniques from nymphing to dry-fly fishing. I mention these things in closing my invitation to you to fish because you should have horizons. Out there in the fishing world are ever more enjoyable challenges. The better fisherman you become, the better you will want to be.

Welcome to fishing!

GLOSSARY OF TERMS

Anadromous Fish: Fish that are born in fresh water, go to salt water for growth to adulthood, then return to fresh water to spawn.

Bait-and-Tackle Store: A store where fishing bait and equipment are sold.

Bait-casting Rod: A short flexible rod used to cast artificial lures using a bait-casting reel.

Bait Box: A box used to hold bait, particularly live bait such as worms and nightcrawlers.

Boat-fishing: Fishing done from a boat, either on freshwater lakes and ponds or on the ocean.

Bobber: Any floating device (usually a cork or plastic air bubble) used on a fishing line to keep bait off the bottom.

Charter: To rent a boat for fishing, either on freshwater lakes or on the ocean.

Cold-water Fish: Fish that need cold water (usually below 80° F) in which to live: trout, salmon, and others.

Downrigger: A short rod, wheel, and cable mounted on a boat and used to sink baits deep into the water.

Drag: Tension placed on the fishing line using a brake on the fishing reel.

Fish-finder: A small box that locates fish through the use of sonar—radio signals sent to the lake or ocean bottom.

Fishing License: A state or federal permit to fish required by most states for adults fishing on fresh water. Most states allow children to fish without a license.

Habitat: The environment in which fish and other animals can survive. In the case of fish, clean water at the right temperature is needed.

Inshore Fishing: Ocean fishing that is done along the shoreline and in shallow ocean waters.

Jetty: A man-made structure (usually of rock) that extends from land into the ocean or lake. Jetties are used to break waves, creating a safe harbor.

Lure: An artificial bait used to imitate food fish eat.

Monofilament: Line made of single-strand nylon.

Nightcrawlers: Wormlike creatures that live in the ground and come out at night in summer to mate.

Offshore Fishing: Deep-water ocean fishing requiring large boats and heavy tackle to fish.

Panfish: Small warm-water fish that live in fresh water ponds and lakes: sunfish, crappie, bluegill, etc.

Predator: A fish or animal that kills other fish or animals for survival food. Most fish are predators.

Rain Gear: Rubber, nylon, or Gore-tex jackets and pants used for protection against foul weather, rain, wind, and cold.

Rig: An arrangement of tackle to catch fish. Different rigs are used for different fish and fishing conditions.

School: A group of fish that swim and act as one. An example is a school of bluefish in the ocean or a school of perch in fresh water.

Set the Hook: Pulling up and back on your rod when a fish strikes to sink the barb (point) of the hook into the fish's jaw.

Sinkers: Round BB-like sinkers are called "split-shot." They come in different weights—heavy for fast currents, big lakes, or ocean uses. Other types of sinkers are "twist-ons," "bell-sinkers," and "slip-sinkers." All are used to get bait down in the water, where the fish are lying or swimming.

Snap Swivels: Wire snaps used to attach lures and hooks to a line. Snap swivels, like sinkers, come in sizes from small to very large.

Spawn: To lay eggs and sperm (milt) to create a new generation of fish. Some fish spawn in gravel, while others "free-spawn," laying eggs in water. Examples of gravel-spawners are trout and salmon. Striped bass and shad are free-spawners.

Spin-fishing: Fishing with a spinning rod and reel.

Spinner: A type of spinning lure that has a blade that spins around a metal shaft.

Spinning Reel: A type of fishing reel most commonly used by fishermen. It has a drum around which is wound monofilament that balloons off the drum when a lure is cast.

Still Waters: Lakes and ponds where the water does not flow noticeably.

Strike: When a fish hits a bait offered by the fisherman.

Surf: Where the waves break onto a beach.

Surf-casting: Casting lures and bait into the surf.

INDEX